Contents

Unsolved mysteries

For centuries, people have been puzzled and fascinated by mysterious places, creatures and events. Is there really a monster living in Loch Ness? Did the lost city of Atlantis ever exist? Are UFOs tricks of the light, or actually vehicles from outer space? Who is responsible for the strange patterns called crop circles – clever hoaxers or alien beings? Some of these mysteries have baffled scientists, who have spent years trying to find the answer. But just how far can science go? Can it really explain the seemingly unexplainable? Are there some mysteries which science simply cannot solve? Read on, and make your own mind up...

This book tells you about the history of crop circles. Using eyewitness accounts and the scientific evidence found in crop circle sites it looks at the different theories about how crop circles form.

What is a crop circle?

You have probably seen pictures of crop circles. They are circular patterns which mysteriously appear in fields of crops, such as wheat and barley. Inside the circle the crop stalks are bent over, but at the circle's edge the crops are untouched. Circles don't last forever – they are destroyed when the crop is harvested. Crop circles are not always single, perfect circles – often, two or more crop circles appear at the same time. Some circles are elliptical (oval shaped); some are complicated designs that crop circle researchers call **pictograms**.

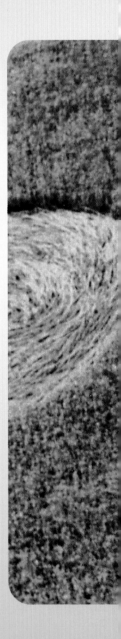

Crop circles first made the news in the early 1980s, when dozens began to appear around the world. Media interest was intense because of claims by UFO enthusiasts that the circles were made by aliens. Crop circles are so neat that they look artificial. In fact, most are, because they are hoaxes! But there are still many which cannot be explained. Is there anything science can do to solve the mystery?

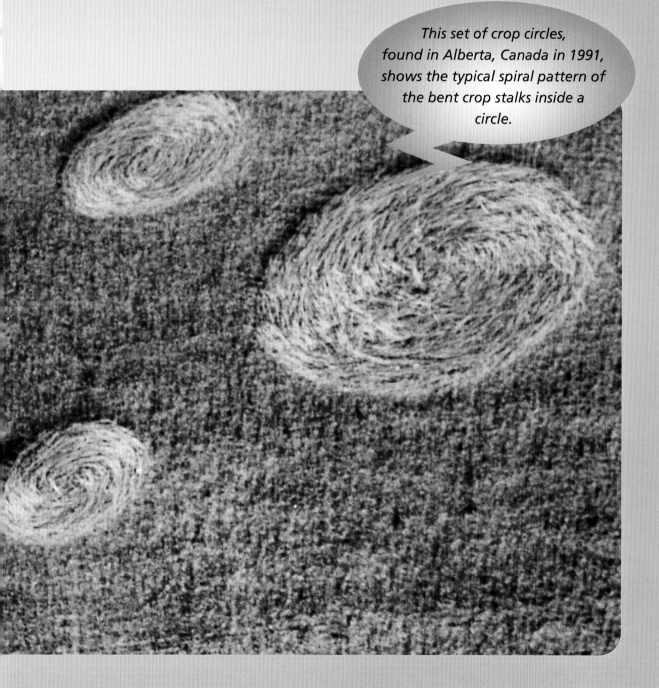

This set of crop circles, found in Alberta, Canada in 1991, shows the typical spiral pattern of the bent crop stalks inside a circle.

The circles appear

Headlines about crop circles first appeared in the world's newspapers and on television in the early 1980s, but this was not the first time crop circles had been seen. There were several reports from Australia, the USA, Canada and England in the 1960s and 1970s, and a few from before that too. The earliest record of a crop circle comes from Holland in 1590. Many farmers had witnessed them before, but had put their appearance down to the wind.

A crop of circles

During the early 1980s, reports of crop circles rose dramatically. Dozens of circles appeared each summer. Most were in the fields of the English **counties** of Hampshire and Wiltshire, and many were concentrated around the town of Warminster, which is also famous for UFO sightings. For a few years, there was huge media attention and plenty of speculation about alien spacecraft landing and little green men making the circles. The hype was made more intense because the film *E.T.: The Extraterrestial*, about an alien left behind by a departing spacecraft, was showing at the time. By the late 1980s, reports of crop circles were coming in from all over the world. In 1990, more than a thousand circles were reported.

An engraving from 1678 appears to show a crop circle. The report with the engraving says that the circle was formed overnight by the 'mowing devil'.

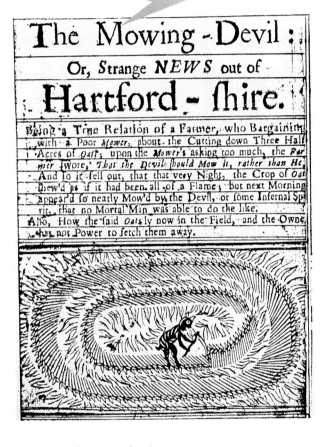

The Mowing - Devil:
Or, Strange NEWS out of
Hartford - shire.

Being a True Relation of a Farmer, who Bargaining with a Poor Mower, about the Cutting down Three Half Acres of Oats; upon the Mower's asking too much, the Farmer swore, That the Devil should Mow it, rather than He. And so it fell out, that that very Night, the Crop of Oat shew'd as if it had been all of a Flame; but next Morning appear'd so neatly Mow'd by the Devil, or some Infernal Spirit, that no Mortal Man was able to do the like. Also, How the said Oats ly now in the Field, and the Owner has not Power to fetch them away.

Modern patterns

In the 1990s, crop circles have continued to appear, but matters have taken a strange twist. Although most reports are of simple circles and groups of circles, complex designs have also been sighted, including squares, triangles, mathematical patterns and even letters. Crop circle researchers call these patterns **pictograms** or **agriglyphs**.

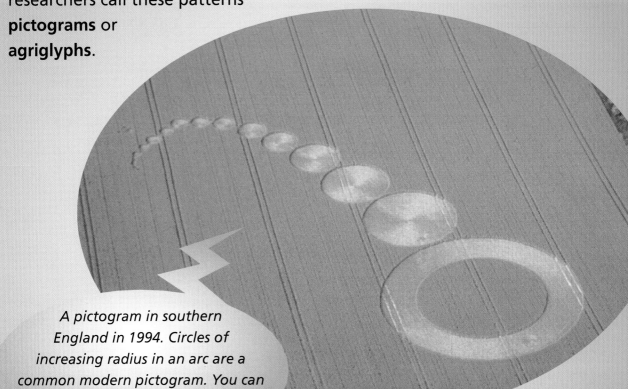

A pictogram in southern England in 1994. Circles of increasing radius in an arc are a common modern pictogram. You can also see the 'tramlines' formed by tractor wheels.

Circles around the world

Most crop circle reports come from southern England, but crop circles have appeared all over the world. They are found in more than 70 countries from every continent, including the USA, Canada, Australia, Japan, France and India. Circles have also been found in many different types of crop around the world, from tobacco to rice. Circle shapes have also been seen in sand and snow.

Did you see that?

Considering the thousands of crop circles which have been discovered in the last 30 years, and that they seem to appear only in certain places, very few people have actually seen them being made. This may be because they seem to appear mostly at night. Of course, many people have seen and photographed the finished circles.

Queensland, Australia, January 1966

George Pedley was driving his tractor through a field of sugar-cane when he saw what he described as a blue-grey spaceship, about 25 metres across, flying out of a swamp about 30 metres away. It dived down, rose again and flew off, spinning all the time. At the spot where he had seen the spaceship rise, Pedley found a 30-metre wide circle where the swamp reeds had been swirled around. He described the reeds as having been 'subjected to some terrific **rotary** force'. He found two more circles close by.

Wiltshire, England, August 1983

Melvyn Bell was riding his horse on the hills on the northern edge of Salisbury Plain. His notice was drawn to dust **spiralling** upwards about 50 metres away in a field of wheat. As he watched, in just a few seconds, a crop circle was formed in the wheat. The dust and a few broken stalks fell from the air around the edge of the circle.

Hambledon, England, August 1990

Gary and Vivienne Tomlinson were walking through fields of corn in the late evening. A light breeze was making the corn sway in waves. As they stood watching, there was a disturbance in the middle of the field and a whistling sound began. What they described as 'a large whirlwind' began to push the corn down. Mini whirlwinds also began forming and disappearing. 'We stood watching in amazement, the corn swirled and then laid down.'

Lights in the sky like this one are sometimes seen at the same time as crop circles are formed. This light appeared in New Jersey, USA, where it is called the 'spook light'.

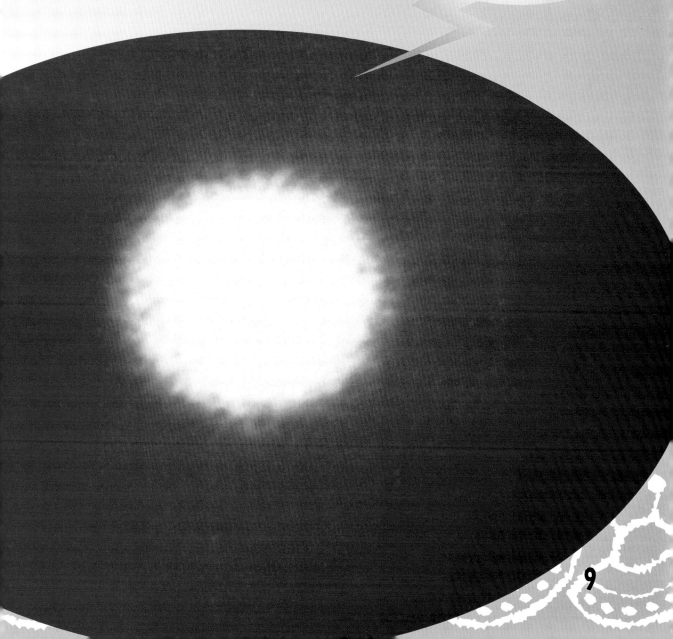

Physical evidence

You know what a crop circle is, but what do they really look like, and what sort of scientific evidence can a crop circle investigator find at a crop circle site?

The size of the circles varies widely – they range from less than a metre up to 50 metres across. The complex formations and **pictograms** are much bigger (see page 13). The crop 'circles' are hardly ever perfect circles, but slightly stretched circles called ellipses instead, and the swirling pattern does not always start exactly in the centre.

British crop circle researcher Dr Terence Meaden measuring a circle formed in Wiltshire, England in 1991.

Edges and swirls

The two most amazing things about a crop circle are its very definite boundary and the accurate **spiral** pattern of the flattened crop stalks. At the circle's edge, the stalks just inside the circle are flattened, and those just outside are untouched.

The crop stalks in a crop circle are bent into a 'swirl pattern'. This is normally a spiral pattern, with the stalks in the centre pointing away from the centre and the stalks at the edge pointing along the **circumference**. Sometimes there are two spiral centres instead of one. Spirals appear circling both clockwise and anticlockwise, and sometimes both ways in patterns which have more than one circle.

Close examination of swirl patterns shows that swirls are not as simple as they first appear. There can be layers of stalks, with the top layer swirling clockwise and the layer underneath swirling anticlockwise.

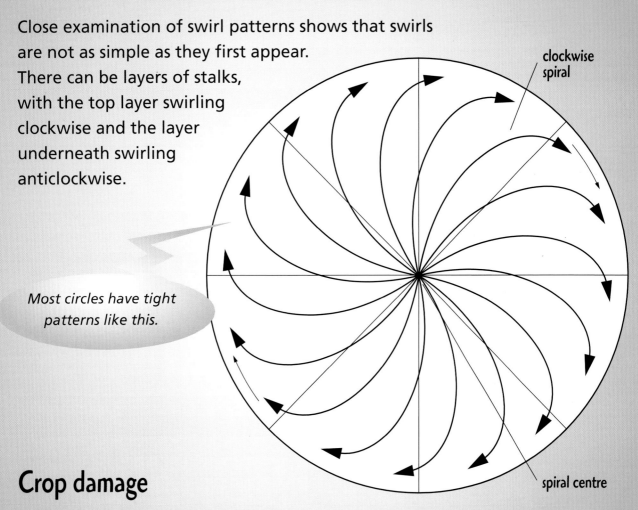

Most circles have tight patterns like this.

clockwise spiral

spiral centre

Crop damage

Surprisingly, most crop stalks inside the circle are not actually broken, but just bent over. Above the bend, the crop is undamaged, and even keeps growing after the circle has appeared.

Circle formations

As we have already seen, crop circles are hardly ever perfect circles. They are often not single or simple circles either. Some circles are formed in groups, some are surrounded by thin crop rings and some have lines leading away from them. Other 'circles' have appeared in the form of complex patterns called **pictograms** or **agriglyphs**.

Basic formations

Several different crop circle formations have been found so far. The most simple formation is the single circle. Some circles are found in pairs (called doublets), groups of three (called triplets) or groups of four (called quadruplets). Other circles have one or two thin rings around them, sometimes just a few centimetres thick.

A quintuplet formation consists of a single circle (with or without a ring) with four smaller 'satellite' circles forming a cross shape. The size of the circles, the thickness of the rings and the distances between the circles can all vary.

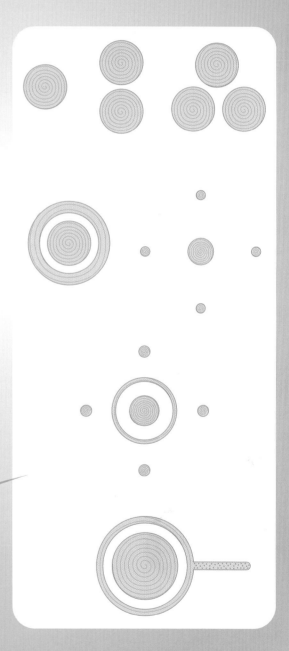

The basic forms of crop circle found so far. The single plain circle is the most common.

Spurs and tramlines

A few circles have a line of flattened crops called a spur leading away from them. The spurs often follow lines in the crop formed by tractor tyres (which are called tramlines). Tramlines are handy for crop circle hoaxers to walk along without damaging the crop.

The famous and extraordinary crop pictogram known as the Stonehenge Julia Set.

Crop pictograms

Since 1990, crop circle formations have become more and more complex and larger and larger (the largest are more than a kilometre long). They are called pictograms or agriglyphs. However, three-quarters of crop circles are still the basic shapes described above.

Formations have also appeared that are based on complex mathematical patterns. One such formation appeared on 7 July 1990 just a few hundred metres from Stonehenge in Wiltshire, England. It was 300 metres across and included 149 separate circles in a mathematical pattern known as a Julia Set, similar to the **fractal patterns** you may have seen drawn by computers.

Evidence on the ground

From the last few pages, you now know that crop circles come in numerous different sizes, shapes and formations, with various patterns made by the crop stalks inside the circles. But what other evidence can be found at crop circle sites, either in the ground or in the crop itself?

The lie of the land

Most, but not all, crop circles appear in fields which are close to the bottom of small but steep hillsides. The direction that the hillside faces, and the direction of the prevailing wind (the direction that the wind blows most often) may be important too. Circles seem to appear when the wind blows over the hill towards the field of crops.

The gentle, rolling countryside of Wiltshire, England. Many crop circles form at the base of these hills.

Energy fields

Researchers have tested the area inside crop circles for **electromagnetic radiation** and **magnetic fields**. Some circles do emit weak radiation for several days after the circle has appeared. Magnetic fields much stronger than the Earth's usual magnetic field have also been found. There are also reports of compasses spinning out of control and electrical equipment failing inside circles.

Hamish Miller is using a **divining** rod to try to find underground features which might be linked to the formation of the crop circle.

Biological evidence

The eminent American **biophysicist** Dr William Levengood has carried out biological tests on wheat stalks from in and around crop circles. He found that the bumps (called nodes) on the bent stalks from inside the circles were enlarged compared to the control stalks (normal stalks from just outside the circle). He suggests that this could be caused by some sort of microwave heating, similar to the way that a microwave oven cooks food. Strangely, there is also some evidence that crops inside circles actually grow better than crops outside, even though they are bent over!

The theories

Many different people have put forward many different theories about what causes crop circles. Some theories are carefully thought out, taking evidence from eyewitnesses and physical evidence from the crop circles themselves. Other theories take little evidence into account and assume things that could never be tested in a scientific way. Yet more theories are plain silly, such as the theory that animals create the circles during courtship displays!

The main problem with solving the riddle of crop circles in a scientific way is the problem of gathering evidence when the crop circle is actually being formed. It is impossible to set up measuring equipment because you don't know exactly where crop circles are going to appear. One of the major theories is that all crop circles are faked. It is certain that many are, and you can read about them on page 24. Another popular theory is that they are linked to UFOs (see page 18).

Here are some other theories...

Underground patterns

Some theories say that crop circles are caused by things under the ground or in the soil. These range from the remains of ancient fields and buildings to bombs left over from the Second World War exploding! There is more about some of these theories on page 20.

You can see the circular pattern of wind created by this helicopter's rotor, but could it cause a crop circle?

Aircraft

One of the early theories was that the circles were made by the **downdraught** from helicopters, but this would not flatten the crop in a spiral or in such a neat circle. Another theory was that swirls of air from aircraft wing tips made the circles, but crop circles don't appear under flight paths.

Atmospheric effects

The theories that have most scientific basis are the ones which say that crop circles are created naturally by spinning air in the atmosphere. You can imagine that a circle could be formed by a **tornado** or a similar effect. See pages 21 and 22 for more on these theories.

The UFO theory

The most popular theory about crop circle formation is that the circles and **pictograms** are made by some type of alien life form. Supporters of this 'UFO theory' think that the circles are either produced when alien spacecraft land and take off, or are drawn by aliens who are trying to communicate with us. Some researchers have even tried to **decipher** the more complex crop circle shapes by comparing them to ancient sign languages such as **hieroglyphics**.

Bright lights photographed over the island of Madeira in 1995. Similar lights have been seen near new crop circles.

For and against

There are a few pieces of evidence to support the UFO theory. The main one is that several eyewitness reports talk of strange lights moving around in the night sky before the discovery of fresh crop circles in the same area the next morning. Another is that the most complex pictograms of the 1990s, if they are not hoaxes, are impossible to explain by any other theory.

Against the UFO theory is the common sense argument that if super-intelligent aliens were trying to communicate with us, drawing crop circles that we don't understand is a pretty strange way of doing it! Circles which are supposed to be landing sites don't make much sense – why would the crop be swirled but otherwise undamaged, and why do the sites keep changing size and shape?

The UFO theory is an attractive one because of its link with science fiction and the unknown, but it relies on belief rather than scientific proof. Of course, the theory is impossible to disprove. There is always the possibility, however small, that UFOs really do exist and are making the circles.

Study groups

There are several organizations which research and study crop circles. Some of their members approach the subject from a scientific point of view, and some, who call themselves cereologists, from a more mystical point of view. Among them are the Centre for Crop Circle Studies (CCCS), the Circles Effect Research Unit (CERES) and Circles Phenomenon Research (CPR). There are several interesting crop circle web sites on the Internet, which you can find using the search term 'crop circles'.

Earth and sky theories

Alongside the UFO theory is the 'Earth energy' theory. This says that crop circles are somehow created by the Earth itself as a message to the human race to stop pollution and habitat destruction. It links in with the **Gaia hypothesis** of James Lovelock, which suggests that the Earth acts like a living being. The theory is supported by mystics, **paranormalists** and some **ecologists**.

The theory also ties in with the fact that many crop circles appear near UFO 'hotspots' and, in England, near ancient religious sites. Supporters of the theory also link the circles to **ley lines**, which they describe as 'energy paths' on the Earth's surface.

Swirling winds

The theory which is based most on science is that crop circles are created not by some sort of paranormal effect, but by some sort of swirling air current which occurs naturally in the atmosphere, called a **vortex**. Examples of vortices are **tornadoes** and whirlwinds. The most obvious pieces of evidence for this theory are the fact that the crop stalks in the circle seem to have been swirled around by a flow of air, and that several eyewitness reports talk about swirling winds and dust.

A fast-spinning tornado vortex reaching down from storm clouds to the ground.

Another argument that leads scientists to think that crop circles are linked to the weather is that circles normally appear in the late evening or early morning during the summer, when the air is often still and warm.

Tornado damage in Texas, USA – far worse and over a larger area than seen at crop circle sites.

Tornadoes

So, could crop circles be formed by tornadoes? Tornadoes do swirl and pick up things from the ground, but there are several reasons why tornadoes cannot be responsible. Firstly, tornadoes only stretch down from enormous thunderclouds, and this sort of weather does not appear in eyewitness reports. Secondly, tornadoes normally cause much more damage than is seen in crop circles.

Whirlwinds and plasma

A whirlwind is a small **vortex** of air. Whirlwinds can be less than a metre across or up to 50 metres across, so they are much smaller than **tornadoes**, which can be hundreds of metres across. They do not descend from thunderclouds as tornadoes do, but rise up from warm ground on hot, still days. Whirlwinds often lift dust from the ground, which is why they are called 'dust devils'. Whirlwinds don't normally stay in one place, but sometimes do. Small vortices are often formed when wind blows over the edge of a hill. You can see similar little **eddies** spinning dust and leaves round when the wind blows past the corner of a building.

This globe is filled with low-pressure gas which becomes a plasma when electricity is supplied to the globe. Touching the globe makes the plasma turn back to gas in some places, giving off a strange glow.

The plasma vortex theory

In the 1980s, Dr Terence Meaden, a leading and respected expert on tornadoes and whirlwinds, and head of the Tornado and Storm Research Organisation (TORRO), based in Wiltshire, England, put forward a theory that whirlwinds and eddies are responsible for crop circles. Not ordinary whirlwinds and eddies, but ones in which the air is **electrically charged**. The charged air is called a **plasma**, and the theory is called the plasma vortex theory. Plasma vortices form from whirlwinds and eddies, and can stay in the air for many minutes before descending to the ground to make crop circles.

Light and sound

The **magnetic fields** and electrical currents caused by spinning plasma can create humming sounds and light. These fields could explain equipment failures inside circles, the biological changes in the crops, and the strange sensations a few eyewitnesses have had, such as their hair standing on end. Glowing lights and humming sounds have also often been reported by eyewitnesses. In fact, the glowing effect, which may make a plasma vortex look like a ball-shaped light in the sky, could be responsible for people reporting UFOs. A plasma vortex also moves about naturally as if under remote control, but can remain in one place for minutes on end.

Famous fakes

There are more crop circle fakes than there are fakes of all other mysterious happenings put together. It's likely that nine out of ten crop circles are a hoax. Here you can find out about some famous hoaxes. On page 26 you can find out the reasons why people faked the circles in question.

Doug and Dave

Easily the most famous crop circle hoaxers of all time are two retired British artists called Doug Bower and Dave Chorley, who are known in crop circle circles as 'Doug and Dave'. In September 1991, Doug and Dave claimed that they had faked more than 200 crop circles in total since 1978, including many which were accepted as the real thing. Doug and Dave also said that they knew several other people who had been faking circles, too. This news created a crisis in the crop circle world. Some 'experts' claimed that they already knew that many circles were faked, but that they also knew of some which were not.

Faking a crop circle

A convincing crop circle can be made by walking in ever-increasing circles, trampling down the crop. By walking along the tramlines, the hoaxers can get to the crop circle site without leaving a trail in the field.

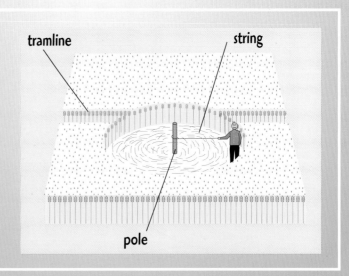

tramline   string

pole

More hoaxers

Rob Irving of Great Britain and an American, Jim Schnabel, also hoaxed crop circles in the summers of 1992 and 1993 to show how easy it is to fake circles. Two more hoaxers, John Lundburg and Rod Dickenson, also fake circles, but own up to the fact, calling themselves crop artists. Dickenson also claims to know who faked the incredible Stonehenge Julia Set, and how they did it.

Media hoaxes

Both television and newspapers have faked circles in an attempt to trick crop circle researchers. In 1991, a British television company faked a crop circle and then asked an 'Earth energy' believer and Dr Terence Meaden to look at it. Both were taken in, saying that it was the real thing. The British newspaper *Today* also tricked one of the leading UFOlogists, Pat Delgado, into saying 'no human' could have made a circle actually faked by Doug and Dave.

Why fake crop circles?

We know that the majority of crop circles are probably faked. But why do people like the famous Doug and Dave fake circles. What is the point? Most fakes are done anonymously, but if nobody knows you did it, why bother? Fame can't be the answer. All a faked circle achieves is to annoy the farmer whose crops are affected.

Some hoaxers fake circles for fun, or perhaps for a dare. There are many stories of agricultural students making circles for a prank. In the 1990s, several hoaxers who make complex **pictograms** have called themselves crop artists, saying that they use fields as the canvas and the crops as their paints. Although they also admit to making some pictograms, they say that they are guided to do so by some **paranormal** force.

As seen from the most famous hoaxes, some circles are faked merely to try to fool crop circle researchers into saying the circles are the real thing. The hoaxers then come clean to show the researchers up as people who don't know a real circle from a fake one. Certain tabloid newspapers have even faked circles to trick other newspapers.

This cartoon from Punch *magazine makes fun of the crop circle phenomenon. This crop circle seems to have been made by a shopping trolley.*

Is it all a hoax?

Some people claim that the whole crop circle **phenomenon** is a huge hoax, and that all crop circles are fakes. Crop circle researchers, whether they believe that the circles are a natural effect of the weather or that they are made by aliens, admit that most circles are fakes, but they are sure that some are real. There are several arguments in their favour. It is very unlikely that all the crop circles around the world could have been faked. Some circles are found away from tramlines with no paths leading to them, so how could they be faked? There are also reports of circles from long before the intense media interest, and eyewitnesses who claim to have actually seen them being made. Many circles appear very close to major roads, where it is unlikely that hoaxers could have faked them without being spotted, even at night.

In conclusion

So can science really solve the mystery of crop circles? Unfortunately, the lack of solid and reliable scientific evidence means that the answer is probably 'no – not at the moment.' Remember that dozens of researchers have studied the circles closely and still there is no conclusive proof. Although many different theories have been put forward to explain crop circles, most can easily be dismissed because they don't match the evidence on the ground.

Is plasma the answer?

The **plasma vortex** theory seems to explain the formation of most crop circles reasonably well, and it does match with what eyewitnesses have seen. Japanese scientists have managed to create small plasma vortices in the laboratory, but the physics of plasma is quite a new science and not really understood yet. Although these experiments prove that plasma vortices exist, this does not prove that they are responsible for crop circles. The main argument against the theory is that it cannot explain the modern **pictogram**-style circles. Supporters of the theory simply claim that these are all hoaxes.

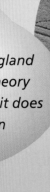

A crop pictogram formed in southern England in 1995. The plasma theory cannot explain this, but it does have the look of an elaborate hoax.

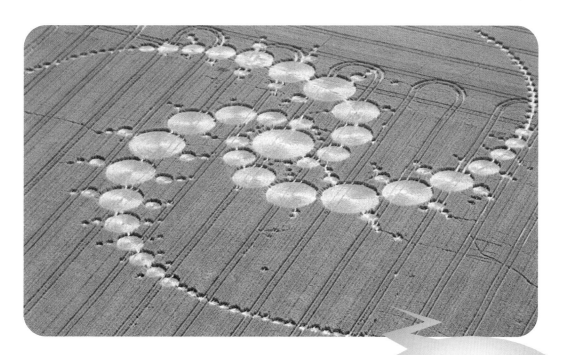

A remarkable modern crop pictogram found (or faked?) in Wiltshire, England.

What do you think?

Now you have read about crop circles
and the possible explanations for them,
can you draw any conclusions? Do you feel that
you can dismiss any of the theories without investigating
them further? Do you have any theories of your own?

What about the UFO theory, or the Earth energy theory?
Can you rule either one out? Perhaps one is the answer, and
it depends on scientific principles that we don't understand
yet. Do you believe that every crop circle is a hoax? Can you
rely on the plasma vortex theory when it is just that – an
unproved theory?

Try to keep an open mind. Bear in mind that if scientists
throughout history had not bothered to investigate
everything that appeared to be strange or mysterious, many
scientific discoveries may never have been made.

Glossary

agriglyph a hieroglyphic shape in the form of flattened crops

biophysics using physics to help study biology, for example, using a knowledge of electricity to understand how nerves work

circumference the edge of a circle, or the distance around the edge of a circle

county an administrative area of the UK

decipher to work out the hidden message in a code of words or pictures

divining finding water or underground objects using intuition or guesswork. Diviners often carry two divining rods, which swing across each other when the water or object is near.

downdraught an air current which blows vertically downwards

ecologist a person who studies the relationship between living things and their environment

eddy a circular movement of air causing a small whirlwind

electrical charge a build up or deficit of electrons (tiny particles which are part of an atom). A build up of electrons gives a negative charge and a deficit of electrons gives a positive charge.

electromagnetic radiation any rays or waves which are part of the electromagnetic spectrum, which includes light rays, radio waves, microwaves, X-rays and nuclear radiation

fractal pattern a mathematical pattern made by repeating the same simple pattern again and again, but moving, rotating and scaling it each time

Gaia hypothesis the theory that all the plants and animals on Earth, together with the seas and atmosphere, act as a huge organism which can change the Earth's environment

hieroglyphics a type of writing which uses simple pictures instead of letters. Hieroglyphics were widely used in Ancient Egypt.

ionized describes an atom which has lost or gained one or more electrons to become electrically charged

ley lines straight lines across the landscape made by ancient tracks or linking ancient monuments, thought by some people to be ancient roads and by others to be lines of mysterious energy

magnetic field the area around a magnet where its magnetic effect can be felt

paranormal describes anything which cannot be explained by scientific investigation. Those who study the paranormal are called paranormalists.

phenomenon a remarkable or unexplained happening

pictogram a simple picture or symbol which represents a word or a phrase

plasma air which has become electrically charged

rotary moving round

spiral a mathematical shape which gets smaller as it moves round, such as the shape on the side of a snail shell

tornado a funnel-shaped spinning cloud which reaches down to the ground

vortex a rotating mass of air or water

Index